BUILDING

AMERICA

The Washington Monument

Craig A. Doherty and Katherine M. Doherty

A B L A C K B I R C H P R E S S B O O K

W O O D B R I D G E , C O N N E C T I C U T

Special Thanks

The authors wish to thank the many librarians who helped them find the research materials for this series—especially Donna Campbell, Barbara Barbieri, Yvonne Thomas, and the librarians at the New Hampshire State Library.

The publisher would like to thank Bonnie Hedges of the Historical Society of Washington, D.C., for her help on this project.

Published by Blackbirch Press, Inc.
One Bradley Road
Woodbridge, CT 06525

© 1995 Blackbirch Press, Inc.
First Edition

Printed in Hong Kong

10 9 8 7 6 5 4 3 2 1

Photo Credits

Cover and title page: ©Everett C. Johnson/Leo de Wys, Inc.
Page 4: photo by William Clark, courtesy National Park Service/U.S. Department of the Interior; page 6: National Portrait Gallery; page 9: National Portrait Gallery; pages 10, 12, 18, 19 (left), 31, 36 : UPI/Bettmann; page 15: National Portrait Gallery; page 19 (right): National Portrait Gallery; page 21: U.S. Department of the Treasury; pages 22, 25, 28, 29, 31, 39: The Historical Society of Washington, D.C.; page 26: Culver Pictures; page 34: National Portrait Gallery; page 40: National Archives; page 41: ©Gabe Palacio/Leo de Wys, Inc.; pages 42-43: ©Everett C. Johnson/Leo de Wys, Inc.

Library of Congress Cataloging-in-Publication Data

Doherty, Craig A.
  The Washington Monument / by Craig A. Doherty and Katherine M. Doherty.—1st ed.
       p. cm.—(Building America)
  Includes bibliographical references (p.) and index.
  ISBN 1-56711-110-6
  1. Washington Monument (Washington, D.C.)—Juvenile literature. 2. Washington (D.C.)—Buildings, structures, etc.—Juvenile literature. [1. Washington Monument (Washington, D.C.) 2. National monuments.] I. Doherty, Katherine M. II. Title. III. Series: Building America (Woodbridge, Conn.)
F203.4.W3D64 1995   94-24477
975.3—dc20   CIP
                                                                                                  AC

Table of Contents

Introduction

George Washington is one of the most beloved figures in the history of the United States. Thirteen states have towns named after him. A New England mountain, a northwestern state, and the national capital bear his name, and his likeness appears on the dollar bill and the quarter. As commander of the Revolutionary War's Continental Army and the first U.S. president, he is one of the founders of our country. Before he died, people were already talking about building a monument to him in Washington, D.C. A space for it was included in the original plans for the city, but it took more than 100 years and nearly $1.2 million to complete the Washington Monument.

At 555 feet, 5 1/8 inches, the Washington Monument is one of the tallest masonry structures in the world. It weighs more than 90,000 tons. At its base it is 55 feet, 1 1/8 inches square. There are 898 steps in the Washington Monument; but, today, most of the more than 1 million visitors a year must ride the elevator up to the top. When riding the elevator, the visitors miss the 193 memorial stones that line the stairway. These stones were donated by 41 different states, 12 countries, 19 U.S. cities, and numerous clubs and organizations.

5

The Debate

Although many people wanted a monument to George Washington as part of the national capital, a debate raged over what form the structure should take. In 1783, the Continental Congress voted unanimously to put a statue of Washington on horseback near the permanent site of Congress. George Washington selected the spot, and Pierre L'Enfant—the designer of Washington, D.C.—included it in his plans. The location was chosen because any structure built there would be visible from all

Opposite: As *the military leader of the Revolutionary War and the first president of the United States, George Washington was truly one of our country's greatest heroes.*

7

over the area. Its closeness to the Potomac River would also make it easy to get materials shipped to the site. Eventually, that is where the Washington Monument was built; however, there was much debate over exactly what should be built there.

After George Washington's death in 1799, some politicians wanted to move Washington's body from his home in Virginia (Mount Vernon) to a tomb in the Capitol building. Congress unanimously passed a resolution to build the tomb. Others felt that, in a republic, no man should be honored above the rest. Also, there were many people who wanted to respect Washington's personal request to be buried at Mount Vernon.

Despite the resolution by Congress, the debate among the various factions prevented any progress from being made on a monument for Washington in the national capital. Other cities—Baltimore, Maryland, and Raleigh, North Carolina, to name two—were able to build memorials to George Washington during this time.

The People Take Over

In 1833, a group of Washington, D.C., citizens, led by U.S. Supreme Court Chief Justice John Marshall, formed the Washington National Monument Society. They wanted to make good on the 50-year-old promise of the Continental Congress. George Watterston, a resident of Washington, D.C., was voted secretary of the Monument Society. Until he died in 1854, he was a driving force in the effort to build the monument. In its first three years, the society was able to raise only $28,000. This was due in part to the fact that John Marshall and the other members of the society limited donations to $1 per person so that all Americans could be a part of building this national memorial. In 1836, when the society felt it had enough money to get started, a much-publicized design competition was held. In publicizing the competition, the society boasted that it would raise $1 million from the people of the United States to build the monument.

In 1833, Supreme Court Chief Justice John Marshall led a group of citizens in the formation of the Washington National Monument Society.

The original design submitted by Robert Mills for the Washington Monument called for an obelisk surrounded by columns and statues.

AN EGYPTIAN SHAPE

The form of the obelisk was created by the ancient Egyptians, who cut them from a single block of stone. Some Egyptian obelisks were more than 100 feet tall and usually had inscriptions covering them. The Egyptians believed that the form of the obelisk was connected to the sun, whose rays widen as they reach the earth, much like the tapered sides of an obelisk. Egyptian obelisks have a pyramidal form at their tops.

The Egyptian obelisks were later valued by Europeans, who, starting with the ancient Romans, brought many of them to Europe. Egyptian obelisks can be seen today in the European cities of Paris, London, Rome, and Florence. There is even one, called Cleopatra's Needle, in New York City.

The design competition was held because the society did not want to follow the suggestion of George Washington Parke Custis, George Washington's stepgrandson. Custis suggested that a burial mound should be built with the work done by people who were descendants of the early settlers in the colonies. Watterston and the other members of the society felt that that would be impractical, and they wanted something more than a large mound.

A number of people submitted designs, but the society was most interested in one done by Robert Mills, a well-known architect of the time. Mills's design was very elaborate. It called for a large structure, built of columns and housing a number of statues, with a 600-foot obelisk (a tall, tapering stone pillar) rising from the center. It is unclear if the society ever considered actually building the entire structure, because from the beginning of the monument's construction, all that was ever attempted was the obelisk.

An Obelisk Rises in Washington

By 1847, the Monument Society had raised $87,000. The money had trickled in from a variety of sources: Census takers earned a twenty percent commission on all donations they collected while carrying out their door-to-door job. The U.S. secretary of the navy asked all sailors to contribute. The U.S. secretary of state suggested that all American consuls solicit donations from Americans living overseas. These and many other fund-raising campaigns made the Washington Monument a truly national project.

On January 31, 1848, Congress passed a resolution giving the Monument Society the 30 acres of chosen land for the project. This cleared the way for construction to begin. Congress did not, however, grant any money to fund the monument's

Opposite:
Construction on the monument began in 1848 and proceeded for five years. In 1853, however, when the structure had reached a height of 150 feet, work stopped due to lack of funds.

construction. The society planned to lay the cornerstone for the monument on Washington's birthday, February 22, 1848. Plans had to be delayed, however, and the ceremony took place on July 4, 1848.

The laying of the cornerstone brought out a sense of patriotism and community spirit among the people of the area. The 24,500-pound marble cornerstone was donated by Thomas Symington of Baltimore, Maryland, who owned a quarry 11 miles from Washington, D.C. The Baltimore and Ohio Railroad transported the stone, free of charge, and a number of workers from the Washington Navy Yard volunteered to help move the huge piece of marble to the monument site.

Matthew G. Emery, a stonemason and contractor, who later became the mayor of Washington, cut and dressed the cornerstone for free. A place for a time capsule was marked in the stone, and two marble cutters, named Dougherty and Berry, made the cutout for free. And yet another Washington businessperson, Clement Woodward, volunteered to make the zinc box for the time capsule. In the same spirit, James Dixon volunteered to be construction superintendent until someone could be hired for the job on a permanent basis.

A number of different objects were placed in the time capsule's zinc box, including a copy of the Declaration of Independence, a copy of the U.S. Constitution, the 1840 U.S. census, the catalog of the Library of Congress, numerous U.S. coins, a copy of Mills's original design for the monument, and a number of popular magazines and newspapers of the time.

With approximately 18,000 spectators on hand, President James K. Polk, along with Vice-President George M. Dallas, most of the members of Congress, and a number of distinguished guests, attended the cornerstone-laying ceremony. The same trowel that George Washington had used in laying the cornerstone for the Capitol was used for the Washington Monument. During the ceremony, Congressman Robert Winthrop of Massachusetts gave a 90-minute speech about American liberty, followed by a presidential reception and fireworks.

The remainder of the foundation was built using smaller, six-to-eight-ton blocks of blue gneiss rock from the Potomac River valley. Because there had been some concern about the ability of the ground to support the massive weight of the monument, the society had brought in a group of experts, which included the designer Robert Mills. After examining the substrata (ground layers underneath the surface) of the area, Mills concluded that the monument would be well supported.

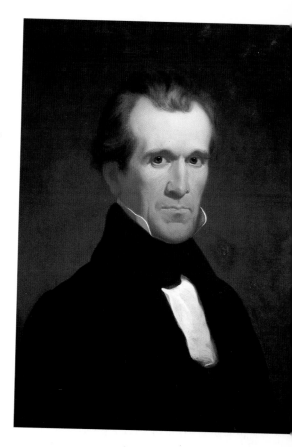

President James K. Polk officiated the cornerstone-laying ceremony for the monument on July 4, 1848.

Stone by Stone

After the ceremonies were over, the work began in earnest. Day by day, the residents of Washington, D.C., and the people across the Potomac in Virginia watched as the monument began to rise. The stone that was used came from a special quarry in Maryland that had supplied the marble for the columns of the Capitol. At times, however, the work had to be stopped because the society had run out of funds.

The stonemasons used a no-mortar technique called "Flemish bond," in which the rectangular blocks of marble are laid with the long side alternating with the short side. In this way, the stones lock themselves together and the weight of the next layer of stone holds the layer underneath in place. Each row of stone added two feet to the height of the structure. Over the next five years, by January 1853, the monument rose to a height of 150 feet before the society ran out of money and had to stop.

Fund-raising was a continuing problem. All sorts of schemes were thought up, but none of them seemed to generate enough money. One success that the society did have was in getting memorial stones to line the inner chamber of the structure. After the state of Alabama offered to send a stone instead of a cash donation, each state (and later other countries and organizations) was asked to donate a native stone 4 feet long and 2 feet thick with a 12-to-18 inch inscription area on its face. The society suggested that the name of the state and its coat of arms should appear on the face of the stone. Eventually, 193 memorial stones were donated and included in the interior surface of the monument. One particular stone—a memorial stone donated by Pope Pious IX—would be at the center of a great controversy for the society.

The Pope's Stone and the Know-Nothings

In 1854, Pope Pious IX sent an original stone from the Temple of Concord in Rome as the Roman Catholic Church's tribute to George Washington. Many people objected to the inclusion of a stone of religious significance in a secular (non-religious) monument. Many newspaper articles suggested the pope's stone be left out, and petitions arrived from around the country objecting to the pope's gift. The most vocal objections came from certain members of the American party, a reactionary political group that was commonly referred to as the "Know-Nothings."

The Know-Nothings had grown in number during the hard economic times of the early 1850s, and their members came primarily from the working classes in the cities around the country. The party blamed the current problems in the United States on the recent waves of Irish and German immigrants. Because party members felt that the United States should be reserved for those people born in this country, they were opposed to the growing presence of "foreign" religions, especially the Catholic Church.

On March 6, 1854, a group of suspected Know-Nothings broke into the Washington Monument construction shed and stole the pope's stone. It is believed that the stone was carried to the banks of the Potomac River and thrown in—it was never recovered. Angered by the incident, the Monument Society fired the monument's night watchman and offered a $100 reward to anyone who helped to capture the thieves.

WHO WERE THE KNOW-NOTHINGS?

In 1849, a secret society called the Order of the Star-Spangled Banner was founded in New York City and gained members quickly. The initiated members were sworn to secrecy. When asked about the group, the members' standard answer was, "I know nothing about it." When the organization went public and became the American party, their critics in the press referred to them as the "Know-Nothings," and the name stuck.

The Know-Nothings grew rapidly into a political force to be reckoned with. Although they often covered themselves in claims of patriotism, they were an organization fueled by bigotry, hatred, and negativism. They felt that the economic changes experienced by the country in the early 1850s were caused by the large number of recent immigrants to the United States. Their suggested solution was to close the borders and send anyone not born in this country back where they came from, especially if they were followers of the Catholic Church.

The Know-Nothings were a secret organization that often met by torchlight at night.

A *Know-Nothing handbill from the 1856 presidential election.*

people that they were serious about completing the monument, two courses (layers) of stone were added while they were running the society. The stone they used had already been discarded as unsuitable, and it had to be removed when construction started up again 25 years later.

The Know-Nothing party's life was quite short-lived. By the 1856 presidential election, their candidate, former president Millard Fillmore, was able to carry only one state. The party had split, like the rest of the country, over the issue of slavery. When southern party members forced a pro-slavery plan into the party's platform, many anti-slavery members abandoned the party.

The Know-Nothings saw the Washington Monument as a symbol of the patriotism they claimed to support. (George Washington, however, probably would have been angered by their intolerance. Nevertheless, they adopted him as their hero and took over his monument.) During the three years they controlled the Monument Society, the Know-Nothings were only able to raise $300. To try and show

Millard Fillmore

No one was ever arrested, and the controversy caused the trickle of contributions to all but stop. The society then appealed to Congress for help. It looked as though Congress would come to the monument's rescue with an appropriation of $200,000, but the Know-Nothings once again got involved.

Members of the Know-Nothing party who had cleverly joined the Monument Society ran a very small ad in local newspapers, calling for a pre-dawn meeting on February 22, 1855, to elect their own officers for the society. The legitimate leaders of the society tried to discredit the Know-Nothings, but it was no use. Displeased by the Know-Nothings' involvement, Congress revoked its promise to fund the monument project. Shortly afterward, on March 3, 1855, Robert Mills died, discouraged that work on the monument had stopped.

For a time, there were two sets of officers who claimed to be in charge of the Monument Society. At first, William Dougherty, superintendent of construction for the society, refused to turn the site over to the Know-Nothings' board. The Know-Nothings, however, were determined to take over, and a large group of party members forcibly controlled the site of the monument on March 9, 1855.

For the next three years, no real progress was made on the project, although the Know-Nothing board had two layers of inferior stone added in an attempt to prove they were serious. When the Know-Nothings gave the monument back to the society in October 1858, great damage had already been done and the society was unable to raise any money.

ROBERT MILLS: AMERICAN ARCHITECT

Robert Mills was born in Charleston, South Carolina, in 1781. His father had emigrated from Scotland and married a woman who was from an established South Carolina family. Mills attended the College of Charleston and then went on to become the first professional architect to be trained in the United States. His predecessors in the field had all been trained in Europe. Mills studied first with James Hoban, the designer of the White House, and then, in 1803, he spent time at Monticello, the home of Thomas Jefferson. There, Mills was treated like a member of the family and was given access to Jefferson's vast architectural library.

With Jefferson's help, Robert Mills spent five years working with Benjamin Latrobe, a noted architect and the U.S. surveyor of public buildings. In 1808, Mills entered into private practice in Philadelphia, where he designed a number of public and private structures. Then,

in 1814, he won the design competition for a Washington monument to be built in Baltimore, Maryland. The Baltimore monument is a tall Greek column with a statue of George Washington on the top.

Before winning the design competition in Washington, D.C., for its monument, Mills had designed a number of buildings in the capital, including the U.S. Treasury Building, the U.S. Patent Office, and U.S. Post Office. Today, there are at least 50 major structures around the country that stand as a reminder of the skill of Robert Mills, America's first homegrown architect.

His death, on March 3, 1855, came at a time when the monument he had designed was at a standstill due to the many ongoing struggles with the Know-Nothing party. Unfortunately, this great champion of the Washington Monument died in deep disappointment and with little hope that his grand marble obelisk would ever be completed.

The U.S. Treasury Building in Washington, D.C., is another famous structure designed by Robert Mills.

3

When Will the Monument Be Finished?

By 1858, when the Monument Society regained control of its project, the country was involved in the slavery debates that would soon lead to the Civil War. Few people were interested in finishing a stalled monument that had been sidetracked by the Know-Nothing controversy. For the next 25 years, the 150-foot-high unfinished monument stood at the center of the nation's capital as a sad reminder of the country's political failures. During the Civil War

Opposite: While construction was underway, a crane on top of the structure pulled the large blocks of marble up to the workers.

23

(1861-1865) the country was bitterly divided into North and South. Repeated attempts at raising monument money at this time failed miserably. During the war, the fields around the monument were used to graze sheep and cattle, which helped to feed the Union army.

In the 1870s, interest in completing the monument again started to grow. The New York legislature, on April 21, 1871, voted to donate $1,000 to the Washington National Monument Society. Then, in 1872, other states followed: Minnesota voted $1,000, New Jersey $3,000, and Connecticut $2,000. A congressional committee studied the situation in 1873 and recommended that Congress fund the completion of the monument. The recommendation, however, was not acted upon by Congress.

Who Wants That Ugly Monument?

By the 1870s, the monument became the center of another controversy—this time over the design. In the more than 30 years since Mills had drawn up the monument, American tastes in architecture had changed to much more ornate styles. Critics of the time saw the bare, stark obelisk as unacceptable. They wanted something more decorative.

The debate broadened to include a public argument over whether a new architect or a sculptor should redesign and finish the monument. About the only point that most people agreed on was that something needed to be done about this obvious failure. Some of the designs suggested at the time had the existing structure turned into an ornate Italian-style tower, an English Gothic tower, or a

Opposite:
This sketch of a revised design for the Washington Monument appeared in the New York Post *in 1879 along with drawings of the project's key men. Influenced by the tastes of the time, this design was much more elaborate than the simple obelisk.*

JOHN McKENNA

JOSEPH FAUNCE

P. H. McLAUGHLIN SUPERINTENDENT

THEODORE RYDER

JAMES EVANS

E. R. WAYSON

JOHN LEWIS

JOHN MALONEY

JAMES HOGAN

CHAS CUMBERLAND

JAMES CHAUNCEY

WM BRANSON

CHARLES SMITH

JOHN FLYNN

JOSEPH ENGELFING

LEWIS O'BRIEN

SAM MASTON

DENNIS O'LEARY

JAMES WELLS

GEORGE KNIGHTSEY

JAMES E. TALBOTT

Romanesque tower. The U.S. Army Corps of Engineers, which had now been put in charge of completing the monument, wanted to find a way just to cap off the obelisk at its current height and be done with it.

Two events finally got the monument back on the right track toward completion: First, Lieutenant Colonel Thomas Casey, of the Corps of Engineers, was put in charge of the project. Second, on

By 1876, a new man— Lieutenant Colonel Thomas Casey of the U.S. Army Corps of Engineers— was formally put in charge of overseeing the rest of the monument's completion.

July 5, 1876—during the country's centennial celebration—Congress suddenly and unanimously voted to
appropriate $200,000 in four annual payments
for the completion of the structure. Congress's plan
called for a monument-completion deadline of
October 19, 1881. This was the 100th anniversary
of General Charles Cornwallis's surrender to General
George Washington at Yorktown, Virginia—the event
that ended the American Revolution. To complete
the deal, the society deeded the 30-acre site of
the monument back to the federal government
and agreed that the completion of the project
would be run by a joint commission made up of
members of Congress and people from the society.
This plan left neither enough time nor enough
money to finish the project, but it did get work
started in the right direction.

Fixing the Foundation

One of the first problems that Casey dealt with was
the foundation of the monument. Along with the
other engineers working with him, he decided that
the original foundation was not adequate to support
the final weight of the obelisk. To strengthen the
support, all of the area around and under the old
foundation was excavated and a concrete foundation
was added. The old foundation had settled unevenly,
and Casey was able to correct this when expanding
the base.

The second foundation constructed by Casey
and his workers was 2.5 times larger than the
original, and it was 13.5 feet deeper. This was
necessary to spread the downward force created

by the structure over a greater area. The work of expanding the foundation cost $94,474 and was completed in 1878. The monument could now be completed safely, if Casey and the commission could ever agree on what to do.

Heated debate still continued on what the final monument should look like. The members of the Monument Society rejected all plans that changed the obelisk into some other form, and the joint commission finally agreed to let the obelisk stand. Then

Under Lieutenant Casey's command, the foundation of the monument was more than doubled in size to insure the structure's stability.

The new foundation was added in sections.

the debate centered on the proportions of the obelisk and what, if any, decorative features should be included.

Casey argued, and eventually got agreement from the commission, for an obelisk that looked as much like a monolithic (one single) piece of stone as possible. The commission agreed with Casey by finally stating that they had no authority to change the original design and could only deal with questions that concerned the actual engineering of the project. Casey was then allowed to re-engineer some of the aspects of the monument in order to make it more sound.

He removed an Egyptian inscription that Mills had designed from above the doorway, made the entrance smaller, and equipped it with a marble door that matched the rest of the stonework. When they eventually got to the top of the monument, the windows were fitted with shutters whose color also matched the stonework. This way, from a distance, the structure would look like a single piece of stone.

The height and top of the obelisk were also subjects in the ongoing engineering debate. Casey corresponded with George Marsh, the U.S. minister to Italy, about the proportions of the Egyptian obelisks in Rome. He learned that the height of an ancient obelisk is ten times the width of its base.

This meant that Washington's obelisk should be 550 feet high (not the 600 feet that Mills had originally called for) since the base is 55 feet wide. The final engineering solution was to follow the existing taper to a height of 500 feet and then top the monument with a 55-foot-high pyramid.

By 1880, *the new foundation was nearly complete.*

MONEY AND THE MONUMENT

One of the great mysteries surrounding the length of time it took to build the Washington Monument was the lack of success that the Washington National Monument Society had in raising money for the project. It seemed that no matter what they tried, the money merely trickled in. The society intended from the very beginning to raise $1 million. It expected great numbers of Americans to contribute because it limited its first fund-raising request to only a $1-donation per person.

In the first three years, however, the society raised a mere $28,000. It then hoped the publicity surrounding the design competition would help to generate more money, but financial hard times in the United States in the late 1830s hurt the fund-raising efforts. By 1847, the fund had reached only $87,000. Despite its noble efforts, the Monument Society could not raise enough money.

During the 1840 U.S. Census, the federal marshals conducting the census were authorized to collect money for the monument and were even offered a twenty percent commission on the funds they collected. The U.S. secretary of the navy assisted the society in a plan to solicit funds from sailors, and the U.S. secretary of state directed U.S. consuls to try and get donations from Americans living abroad. Appeals also went out to schoolchildren, churches, and other organizations.

The wives of James Madison, John Quincy Adams, and Alexander Hamilton organized women to help with the fund-raising. Several well-known politicians of the day—John Quincy Adams, Henry Clay, Millard Fillmore, James K. Polk, Zachary Taylor, and Daniel Webster, to name a few—tried to help, but were not too successful.

Prints were made of Robert Mills's winning design and were offered as gifts to those who would donate, but still the money only trickled in. When the Know-Nothings took over the monument between 1855 and 1858, they were able to raise only $300 in three years. The controversy created by the Know-Nothings made it almost impossible for the legitimate members of the Monument Society to raise money once they were back in control of the monument.

The Civil War came in 1861 and put the monument project on hold for more than a decade. Finally, Congress did what it had failed to do since the first plan to build a Washington monument was passed in 1783: They appropriated $200,000 in 1876 and set the stage for completing the monument that would forever pay tribute to America's greatest hero.

When the monument was completed in 1885, the total cost had been recorded at more than $1.1 million. The Washington National Monument Society, despite its dedicated efforts, had paid for less than $300,000 of the project's expenses.

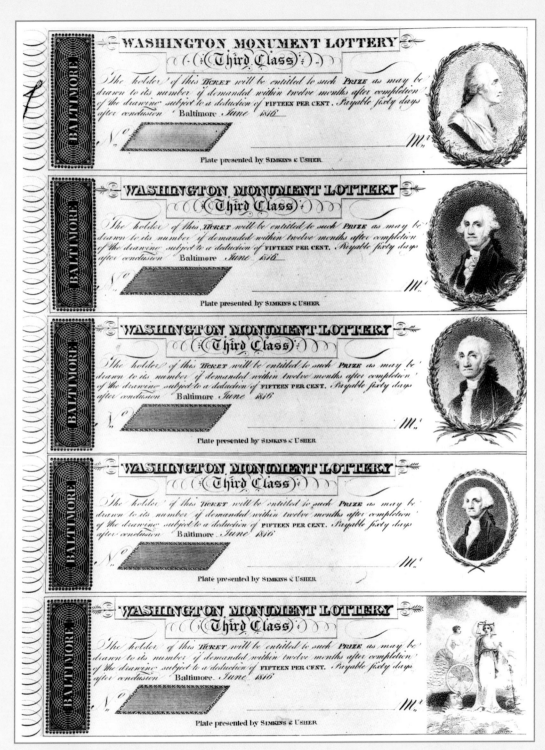

Various efforts to raise money were made all across the country. These Washington Monument lottery tickets were issued by a firm in Baltimore, Maryland.

Elevators and Electric Lights

In the summer of 1880, with the foundation newly strengthened, Casey turned his attention to raising the obelisk. Technology had advanced since work stopped in the early 1850s, so rather than build a new system of ropes and pulleys to lift the stones, an elevator was built inside the structure. Electric lights were also installed to light the inside of the shaft. Although installed to aid in construction, the elevator has remained an integral part of the monument. Today, it lifts millions of tourists to the top each year.

With the elevator ready to carry supplies up to the workmen, Casey had one last task to perform before construction could begin anew: The two courses (layers) of inferior stone raised by the Know-Nothings had to be removed. On August 7, 1880, a second cornerstone-laying ceremony was held when President Rutherford B. Hayes rode up the elevator and placed a small coin in a patch of mortar. He also wrote his initials and the date in the wet cement, and the first stone in more than 25 years was added to the monument.

Not only had technology advanced by this time, ideas about safety had also progressed. With the renewal of construction, a safety net was added to the outside of the monument and moved up as the obelisk grew. Although no injuries were reported in the building of the structure, there are reports that more than one worker fell into the safety net.

The next problem Casey faced was finding marble that would match the stone originally used in the first 150 feet. Casey and the commission contracted

President Rutherford B. Hayes attended the monument's second cornerstone-laying ceremony on August 7, 1880. The second ceremony marked the beginning of work that had been left untouched for nearly 25 years.

with a Massachusetts quarry for stone and they were able to complete 13 courses (or 26 feet) of the structure before the quarry defaulted on its contract. At this point, they arranged to get the rest of the marble from a quarry in Maryland. At first it appeared that all the marble used throughout the monument's construction matched quite well, but as the stone weathered, the Massachusetts stone changed color slightly. Today, there is a visible ring around the middle of the monument created by the different-colored marble from Massachusetts.

4

Up, Up to the Point

Once work began in 1880, the monument grew steadily during the working season. In that year, 26 feet were added; then, in 1881, 74 more feet. In 1882, 90 feet were added; a total of 70 feet went up in 1883, along with 90 feet in 1884. As the stonework went up, Casey added a slight twist to the obelisk so that the four faces would line up with the four directions of the compass—north, south, east, and west.

On August 9, 1884, the last stone was set at the 500-foot level and work finally began on the

Opposite: On December 6, 1884, a special aluminum cap was placed on top of the Washington Monument. The ceremony, which marked the completion of the structure, was held in gale-force winds.

37

pyramid-shaped top ("pyramidion") of the monument. Casey and the commission wanted something special for the very top of the monument, and they decided to cast a solid piece of aluminum to cap the pyramidion. The 9.5-inch by 5.5-inch, 100-ounce pyramidion cap cost $225 to create and was the largest piece of aluminum ever cast at that time.

Because aluminum was a newly exploited mineral, the pyramidion cap was highly unusual for its era. Before it was set in place, it was displayed in New York and Washington, where viewers asked to step over the small aluminum pyramid so they could later claim that they had "stepped over the top of the Washington Monument," the tallest human-made structure in the world.

The aluminum cap was placed on the obelisk on December 6, 1884, more than 100 years after the Continental Congress had first voted to build a monument to America's first president. In a gale-force wind, six people, including Colonel Casey, climbed up onto the scaffolding surrounding the top of the monument. When they reached the top, a salute was fired and the pyramidion was secured to the top. On the ground below, the rest of the workers and a large number of spectators cheered. A good deal of work was still needed to complete the inside of the structure, but as far as the public was concerned, the Washington Monument was finally finished. The official dedication would be held on Washington's birthday in 1885.

Although the monument would not be open to the public until 1888, President Chester A. Arthur led the list of dignitaries present at 11:00 A.M.,

February 22, 1885, for the official dedication. After the ceremony at the monument, another ceremony and reception was held at the U.S. House of Representatives. The celebration ended after dark with a huge fireworks display.

The topmost piece of stone for the monument was triangular in shape.

The Washington Monument has served as the backdrop for many important events in America's history. In August 1963, more than 200,000 people gathered in front of the monument to hear the Rev. Martin Luther King deliver his famous "I Have A Dream" speech for civil rights.

The Public's Monument

In the end, the Washington National Monument Society had raised only $300,000, and the final bill for the project had exceeded $1.1 million. The other $800,000 had come from Congress. Although many had been reluctant to help the society in its fight to build the structure, as soon as the monument opened in 1888, people came in large numbers to see it. Between August 9, 1888, and January 1, 1903, more than 2.2 million people rode the elevator to the top of the giant white obelisk. Today, more than 1 million people a year visit the Washington Monument, making it one of the most popular attractions in the nation's capital. Tall and elegant, it stands as a dramatic and stirring reminder of one of the greatest heroes in American history.

KEEPING UP THE MONUMENT

Since the completion of the Washington Monument in 1885, little has been needed to maintain the structure. In 1934, workers cleaned the face of the obelisk using wire brushes and a mixture of sand and water. The procedure took five months and cost more than $100,000. In 1994, the monument received a total renovation, which cost more than $500,000 and took almost an entire year.

During the 1994 renovations, workers discovered an area of old graffiti behind some marble in the lobby of the monument. The graffiti, which dates from the 19th century, consisted mostly of some crude drawings. There was also one long message, signed with the initials B.F.B., that reads:

> Whoever is the human instrument under God in the conversion of one soul, erects a monument to his own memory more lofty and enduring than this.

The U.S. Park Service decided, although they had no idea who B.F.B. was, to preserve this section of graffiti and to make it accessible for viewing by visitors.

Other than the graffiti, the only problem the monument has faced involved lightning. It was struck on April 1, 1885, slightly damaging one stone. Although the structure was not really affected, the electrical equipment inside the monument sustained serious damage and much of it had to be repaired or replaced.

The monument was completely renovated in 1994.

The Washington Monument today stands as one of America's most unique and recognizable landmarks.

GLOSSARY

architect A person trained to design buildings and other structures.

census The counting of people in an area. Every ten years, the U.S. government conducts an official census that attempts to count every person in the country.

construction superintendent The person who is in charge of a building project.

cornerstone The first stone laid in the foundation of a structure. Often the laying of a cornerstone is marked with a celebration.

course A layer, referring to stonework.

Flemish bond The technique of laying stones or bricks where every other brick is laid in the opposite direction—that is, the first stone would be set with its long side out and the next stone would be set with it short face showing.

foundation The underlying stone or concrete that is meant to support a structure.

gneiss rock Rock that was created in layers.

graffiti Writing or illustrations that deface an area.

inscription A saying or quotation carved into a plaque or a structure.

Know-Nothings A short-lived U.S. political party also called the American party, most active in the 1850s.

marble A form of limestone that has crystallized over time and formed a hard, close-grained rock.

monolithic Made from one solid piece of material (particularly stone), or designed to appear like one solid piece.

mortar A material that is used to bind masonry together. A mixture of sand, cement, and water is the most common mortar used.

obelisk A tall, tapering structure first built by the ancient Egyptians.

pulley A wheel of various sizes that is used to give a person or machine a mechanical advantage when lifting a heavy object.

pyramid A structure with an equal-sided base (usually a square) and triangular sides that rise and meet at a point. The earliest known pyramids were built as tombs by the ancient Egyptians.

quarry A place where rock is removed from the earth to be used in the construction of various structures.

secular Non-religious.

shutter A device used to cover a window.

time capsule A sealed container or device that is included in a structure or buried by itself. It contains items of the time, intended to be opened sometime in the distant future.

trowel A flat, pointed tool used to spread mortar.

Union The northern states that remained loyal to the U.S. government during the Civil War.

U.S. Army Corps of Engineers A branch of the military that is responsible for overseeing and building a wide variety of public and military construction projects.

zinc An elemental metal.

CHRONOLOGY

1783 August 7—Continental Congress passes resolution to erect a statue of George Washington on horseback.

1791 Pierre L'Enfant includes a site for the Washington statue in his plans for Washington, D.C.

1799 December 14—George Washington dies and is buried at Mount Vernon, his Virginia estate. **December 24**—Congress unanimously votes to build a tomb for George Washington as part of the Capitol building.

1833 Washington National Monument Society is formed to erect a memorial to George Washington.

1836 Monument Society holds a design competition.

1845 November 20—Robert Mills's design is selected as the winner.

1848 January 31—Congress passes resolution deeding 30 acres of land to the society for the monument. **July 4**—Cornerstone of monument is laid and construction starts.

1853 Monument reaches height of 150 feet before construction stops due to lack of funds.

1854 March 6—A stone donated by Pope Pious IX is stolen from the monument site, allegedly by members of the Know-Nothings.

1855 Congress considers funding monument completion of the Washington Monument. **February 22**—Know-Nothings hold elections and take over the Monument Society. They control the project for three years.

1858 October 20—Know-Nothings lose control of the monument and the original society members take control, but bad publicity about Know-Nothings makes it almost impossible to raise any money.

1858–1879 No work is done on the Washington Monument.

1876 July 5—Joint resolution passes both houses of Congress, appropriating $200,000 to be spent on the completion of the monument. The Monument Society returns the monument-site land to the government.

1878 Lieutenant Colonel Thomas Casey, of the U.S. Army Corps of Engineers, is named engineering officer in charge of Washington Monument. **Foundation** is enlarged and strengthened. **Design** changes are proposed.

1880 Elevator is installed. **August 7**—President Rutherford B. Hayes officiates at the laying of a second cornerstone.

1880–1884 Construction work progresses toward completion of the monument.

1884 August 9—Monument reaches height of 500 feet, and the construction of the pyramidal top begins. **December 6**—Aluminum pyramidion cap is set on top, and the exterior of the monument is completed.

1885 February 22—Formal dedication of the Washington Monument is held.

1888 Washington Monument is opened to the public.

1888–1903 More than 2.2 million visitors ride the elevator to the top of the monument.

1934 Exterior of the monument is cleaned using wire brushes and a solution of sand and water.

1994 Monument undergoes a complete renovation.

FURTHER READING

Ayer, Eleanor. *Our National Monuments.* Brookfield, CT: Millbrook Press, 1992.

Boring, Mel. *Incredible Constructions and the People Who Built Them.* New York: Walker & Co., 1985.

Morgan, Sally and Morgan, Adrian. *Structures.* New York: Facts On File, 1993.

Osborne, Mary P. *George Washington: Leader of a New Nation.* New York: Dial, 1991.

Reef, Catherine. *Washington,* D.C. New York: Dillon, 1990.

Steins, Richard. *Our National Capital.* Brookfield, CT: Millbrook Press, 1994.

Williams, Brian. *George Washington.* North Bellmore, NY: Marshall Cavendish, 1988.

SOURCE NOTES

Ayer, Eleanor. *Our National Monuments.* Brookfield, CT: Millbrook Press, 1992.

Cunliffe, Marcus. *George Washington: Man and Monument.* New York: New American Library, 1982.

Early, Eleanor. *Washington Holiday.* New York: Prentice-Hall, 1955.

Freeman, Robert Belmont. "Design Proposals for the Washington National Monument." *Columbia Historical Society Records,* v 49, 151-186.

Gallagher, H. M. Pierce. *Robert Mills, Architect of the Washington Monument, 1871-1855.* New York: Columbia University Press, 1935.

"George Washington's Monument." *American Heritage,* 1968, 70-73.

Griswold, Charles L. "The Vietnam Veteran's Memorial and the Washington Mall." *Critical Issues in Public Art: Content, Context and Controversy.* New York: Harper Collins, 1993, 71-100.

Gutheim, Frederick. "Who Designed the Washington Monument?" *AIA Journal,* v 15, n 3, March 1951, 136-141.

Harvey, Frederick L. *History of the Washington National Monument and Washington National Monument Society.* Washington, D.C.: U.S. Government Printing Office, 1903.

Holt, Michael F. "The Politics of Impatience: The Origins of Know-Nothingism." *Journal of American History,* v 60, n 2, September 1973, 309-331.

Huxtable, Ada Louise. "The Washington Monument." *Progressive Architecture,* v 38, n 8, August 1957, 141-144.

Savage, Kirk. "The Self-made Monument: George Washington and the Fight to Erect a National Monument." *Critical Issues in Public Art: Content, Context and Controversy.* New York: Harper Collins, 1993, 5-32.

"Theological Graffitti Found in Monument." *New York Times,* July 17, 1994, 18.

INDEX